PowerKids Readers:
Nature Books™

Flowers

Jacqueline Dwyer

The Rosen Publishing Group's
PowerKids Press™
New York

Published in 2001 by The Rosen Publishing Group, Inc.
29 East 21st Street, New York, NY 10010

First Edition

Book Design: Michael de Guzman
Layout: Felicity Erwin, Nicholas Sciacca

Photo Credits: pp. 1, 9 © FPG/David McGlynn; pp. 5, 7, 11, 13, 15, 21 © SuperStock, Inc.; p. 17 © Earth Scenes/Richard Shiell; p. 19 © Earth Scenes/Donald Specker.

Dwyer, Jackie, 1970–
    Flowers / by Jacqueline Dwyer.
        p. cm.— (PowerKids readers nature books)
    Summary: A simple description of what flowers are and how and where they grow.
    ISBN 0-8239-5677-6 (lib. bdg.)
    1. Flowers— Juvenile literature. [1. Flowers.] I. Title.

SB406.5. D89 2000
635.9—dc21   99-049973

Manufactured in the United States of America

Contents

Flowers are plants that bloom, or open. Flowers are many colors, shapes, and sizes.

Tulips are closed at night. Most flowers are open during the day. They close up at night when it is dark. Tulips are flowers that open and close.

7

There are lots of tiny seeds inside every flower. The seeds fall to the ground when the flower dies. In the spring, the seeds will grow into new flowers.

Roses grow on a bush.
A rosebush is a plant that
lives for many years.
Some flowers live for one
year. Other flowers live
for many years.

11

Some flowers grow in water. Water lilies are big flowers that float on water.

Some flowers grow on top of tall mountains. These mountain flowers are small. They grow close to the ground.

15

Some people grow
flowers inside a special
building. This building is
made of glass. It is called
a greenhouse.

17

You can grow flowers at home, too. All flowers need water and sunlight to grow.

Pretty flowers make people happy.

21

Words to Know

FLOWERS

GREENHOUSE

MOUNTAIN

SEEDS

WATER

Here are more books to read about flowers:
Flowers (Picture Science)
by Joy Richardson
Franklin Watts

*The Flowers: An Ecology Story Book
(The Ecology Series)*
by Chris Baines
Crocodile Books

To learn more about flowers, check out these Web sites:
http://www.suite101.com/welcome.cfm/kids_gardening
http://www.parentsplace.com/fun/gardening

Index

Word Count: 170

Note to Librarians, Teachers, and Parents

PowerKids Readers (Nature Books) are specially designed to help emergent and beginning readers build their skills in reading for information. Simple vocabulary and concepts are paired with photographs of real kids in real-life situations or stunning, detailed images from the natural world around them. Readers will respond to written language by linking meaning with their own everyday experiences and observations. Sentences are short and simple, employing a basic vocabulary of sight words, as well as new words that describe objects or processes that take place in the natural world. Large type, clean design, and photographs corresponding directly to the text all help children to decipher meaning. Features such as a contents page, picture glossary, and index help children get the most out of PowerKids Readers. They also introduce children to the basic elements of a book, which they will encounter in their future reading experiences. Lists of related books and Web sites encourage kids to explore other sources and to continue the process of learning.